Soul Sanskrit

Awakenings and Meditations of the Soul

By Indi Writes

Poetry

First Printed in United Kingdom 2018

Published by Conscious Dreams Publishing

www.consciousdreamspublishing.com

ISBN: 978-1-912551-25-5

Contents

Dedication

To the moon of my womb
Angel Scar,
and the Sun of my Soul
Ezai White.

Acknowledgements

My sister Nadinha Dias who exposed me to beautiful poetry at an early age.

Michael White, my husband, my boyfriend and dearest friend who always supports me through every decision and outcome.

Nadia Maddy, my very first book coach, author of ***The Palm Oil Stain*** and friend who inspires me and always supports my work.

Danni Blechner, the Book Journey Mentor, who assisted me with publishing ***Soul Sanskrit*** and her team from Conscious Dreams Publishing in London, UK.

Claire Lockey for designing and creating my press release, advertising material and writing the about the author section.

Thank you all.

Using Poetry for Healing

Meditation derives from the Latin word '*mederi*' which defines healing and/or remedy.

Healing emotionally and mentally leads us to heal physically.

Both creation and destruction take place in the mind before it's manifested physically; equally, so does healing and disease.

Your mind is the secret ingredient which makes all things work – or not!

Hopefully, at this point, you have your mind and lucky you to have the Soul Sanskrit too!

Follow these simple instructions to enhance your poetry healing experience.

For best results, smudge yourself with Sage, Rue or incense prior to reading the poems. This is to enhance their meaning as well as your own ability to grasp the essence, truth and healing. Try this especially before the following poems: "Namaste" and "All is all (Cleansing bath)".

When you are anxious, spend five minutes meditating before reading these poems, or at least give it a go. Sit up with your back straight, take a slow deep breath, exhale, then repeat. Continue breathing in and out observing the journey that the air takes inside your body to keep you alive. Then proceed to read: "Wanting", "Birds lessons" and "Labyrinth of the Cellf".

For traumas, blockages and deep-rooted hidden issues, light up a candle, smudge yourself with Sage, Rue or incense then. Take a few deep breaths and proceed to read the following: "Hidden Brokenness", "Let's just be instead of trying to be anything" and "Indigo Maze".

Reading poetry for healing is great. Do I need to say writing it is even better!??

If you desire to heal yourself, writing poetry is a wonderful way to release.

When we release, we are able to clearly see what our own blockages are. We become more accepting and understanding of our suppressed emotions.

Read your poems out loud and share with friends. Write from the heart. Let the pen the paper and all the things you can't explain in your head and heart be released naturally as you experience the healing power of Poetry in your life.

To all my beloved readers, I wish you Peace. I wish you Poetry.

Indi Writes

Dreams are a preview of the Wonderful things that may just happen!
Thanks to the dream giver!!!

On the dark days when only the dead awakens,
I sit here seeking this light
Rolling these papers...
Rolling my life away...
I long for your highest
and I am willing to do whatever it takes.
To crumble you...
With my fingers, prepare you
It is a ritual – and to finalize my experience
I will burn you to test just how real your comfort is.

I have been through storms trying to find You,
Survived wars looking for Your comfort
Now that it's time to let the past go
I realize you are nothing but an element of my imagination...
The Perfectness and Greatness I seek not even I own!

The Art of Love

It's those we love that will hurt us most...

Love is Pure, innocent, transparent...

And we are only humans, learning our ways, learning to love while loving anyhow...

Love is the greatest weapon yet a cobra with two heads...

And true love is the antidote for her venom...

True Love is detached, begins with the self and reflects itself onto others & everything it touches...

Like Magic... Light Magic...

The Heart of Love

Wanting

Are you aware of the value of the water you drink?

Wash, waste, flush...

If you didn't earn it, what makes you deserving?
Or worse, demanding!

Wanting; wanting; wanting

Are you capable of valuing the fabrics you wear?
Which protect your skin, keep you warm?
Giving us sense of dignity, inequality and respect!
Do you understand the cost of its thread?
We go on demonstrating love through diamonds,
Ignoring entirely its bloodshed...

Still wanting; wanting; wanting

Are you aware of its cost, its value?
Did you earn the water which sustains your life?
Did you love back the earth?
How do you plan on paying her back?
Mother Nature indeed is deserving of all,
Dignity; equality and respect.

But we're just wanting; wanting; wanting

Using and abusing this dust that makes up our essence...

What are you wanting; wanting; wanting!?

When gratitude is the greatest tool.
The map to an oasis of abundance.

Are you grateful for the pains and aches?
For the salt in your tears...?
The metal in your heartache...?

For as long as you are wanting; wanting; wanting
You will be waiting; waiting; waiting
While I wait for you to find your worth
Hear the ground yearning for us to pay back her dust.

Will I ever earn enough to want?

Mother Nature – you be my judge!

Sinner Self

Oh, Sinner I love you
Oh, murderer I love you still
Put your hands up
No defence come talk to me
Yes you – carrier of viruses
Contaminator of diseases
Sit awhile beside me
You too – abuser, coward and bully
You are my people
So, come and have a sip
Of my truth tea
Sinner, rebel of your own rules
Murderer of your own dreams
Oppressor of your own children's path
Your viral disease lingers and feeds
The lies and fears
Abuser of your own self
Cowardly cursing, complaining
Spreading seeds of hate
Can you blame you?
When you know and carry all cuts and sores
Ignored
Unattended
Only you will ever know
& Eye, your sister
So, shine on their hate

Take no blame
For it is only your own hate reflected
Pain reflection of your own
Doubled when projected
The way I love you...
Yes you
You who knows not
Thyself yet

Building Society

Would you build an empire upon a sand foundation?
Would you sow your seeds upon concrete?
What makes you think your efforts will strive?
In a diseased society?
What makes you blind to the fact
That until you heal
Whatever you build, it's going to crack
What keeps you going like a mouse on its wheel???
On your knees eyes closed
Not a clue of who's building
But ya'll love the wheel
Ya'll feed, ya'll greed and teach ya'll kids it!!
What good is it you build your house upon a firm strong base
When your whole life was built upon illusions…?
For as we continue to chase out there
We keep dismissing and repressing the power within
What's right here…
Acquiring habits, programming the self
Not even knowing
The half of what we're capable of…
Anything outside of Nature
Is whatever our minds create it to be…
Breathe deep
And know Thee
Build Thyself upon concrete

Fit in Wilderness

Being human is draining on my soul
All these physical needs, habits, addictions… all these feelings
Society, Civilization is the worst wilderness
Not based on survival but greed…
It's more common to steal & kill
Cutting trees
Ignore the essence to create your so called rich?!
Who are these souls?
I don't belong – I take no part in this
Say what you will
It's clear we sprouted from different places
So obvious we have different purposes
I desired to experience physical existence
Instead of constantly strive to be what's expected
The more I find me, the less I fit in

Indigo Maze

Embark into your inner maze
Make the destination be Your Soul
One must leave all 'wanting' behind
It takes practice
Best believe it takes time
Our best efforts may prove failed
Just remember you have no idea of what to expect
Create no further illusions
Take every moment for what it is
You shall find & know everything
The fulfilment of the Soul
May take many lives
We have until infinity
Rest assured there is no deadline
Your perfect flow mystically enhances your glow
Once we let go
We realise we're already everything
We were striving for...
Perfection
Peek

Awaken Still Ain't Free

I am awake, but Eye ain't free...
I changed the sin I was feeding my Soul through these lips with
I shifted all those expired people from where they no longer belong
I switched off the brainwashing box and decalcified my pineal gland...
I abandoned external validation to embrace such solitary knowledge of the Self...
The awakening drove me to do these things...
In hope Eye would find liberty
Yet, the more thy Eye opens...
The more chains attached to me become exposed before me...
So, I repeat...
I am awake, so how can I miss the reality these chains bring??
Eye wide open... Still Eye ain't free!!!
Flesh fasted for 4 years and Eye still hear these chains ring
Like Tibetan bells keeping me in a trance
I ain't going, I ain't staying
But my Eye ain't missing a drip of it...
I am awakened, yet not immune to this mental slavery...
Ever envied the peace of the sleeping sheep, as you go through your torture?
I am Woke yet not excused from my own penalty!
The awakening stage will show you all the chains
I am awake yet – still not free...
This mental conspiracy is suffocating me,
Awake in chains – Nothing will stop me from
Becoming thy Key

Hidden Brokenness

My heart is broken
I felt this lonely before...
I have lived this lonely supressed all along!
Can't state for sure...
As a child who cried for love...
Rocked the fears – tended to things...
Smiled with hidden eyes...
A room, a bed – safe place to call home
A burdened child
I was such a burden...
There's times I become that burden onto myself
Each line I write, cuts, scrapes, reaps for deliverance
Always looking at the brighter side
Though over here hurting
Darkness is a must!
I'm not that little girl anymore
But crying this pain
It's her I hear sob...
Help me Universe
Nature ground me entwine me in my path
Surrender showers of love, peace, prosperity
All over me...
I surrender the truths, I face the lies
I lay awakened and walk in my sleep
As I did...
Healing goes deeper than tears
It's infused in the salt released...

Not every poem brings the answer
Just how not every lover fulfils the desire of comfort
Writing is just like air
Flowing through us, feeding, healing us
Ever so faithfully, consistently we misunderstand...
The simplicity of releasing...
Eye wish you air, I wish you poetry beloved

Depths of the Within

... Paralyzed by this constant idea
In the back of my head hiding its fear
Under this strong face I see, when I look in the mirror

Me? Afraid of fear? – Instead I use reason

Within the one who gets up and never gives up
Within the soul in control
There's a lingering fear...

Multiplying; continuously striving

To take over my soul and all that I own...

Every weakness is an opportunity to be transformed into a strength
If you let it...
Just as for every seed we bury, has an opportunity for growth
If you water it...

Birds' Lessons

Do the birds worry about tomorrow?
Do they mind what feathers they have on their body?
Do they have a law or religion to follow?
One thing I do know is: they fly!
Aren't they're scared in case they fall and die!!?
Don't they ever need an assurance?
From a higher source?
From high above!?
Perhaps not
maybe that's what keeps them flying
So high...
They fly away each day that goes by
Ready to fly and survive till tomorrow
While I sit here longing to fly so high
Wondering, what is it that I want to fly away to?
Do birds ever need a sense, feel of fulfilment?
Do you...?

Labyrinth of the Cellf (Self)

If I am who Eye say I am
The delivery is inevitable
It is not what I know or do
Is who Eye am
An infinite Source of Energy
Able to transmute into whatsoever serves me
But most importantly
Equally serves the universe
From earthly dust
To start dust
Back to the ground again…
Ever so grounded
Levitating beyond
Highnesses above our knowledge

What is knowledge to its Creator?
Whilst as creatures we seek it
Only its maker has mastered it easily
How one would clean a spider web
The clouding
Destruction which comes
With the storm!
Is the mental web
The spider self creates
Surrounding, enslaving the self…
What is a prison

When each prisoner holds the key to their cell??!
Only you know the secret
The way, the path the road
To free yourself

So beloved

Let's just be, instead of trying to be anything

Just as you light up a candle
The flame just burns
Produces light, heat
Does what it does
Naturally. Simply. Mystically.
Serves its purpose, its energy
In this realm of existence for the time being...

Just as the candle gets lit
So do we, likewise we live
Produce our light and love
Oh we love!!!
Do what we do
Naturally. Simply. Mystically.
Serving our purpose, our breaths
In this realm of existence for the time being...

Awakening the Self
Penetrating all those spider webs
Overwhelming gratefulness

Looking at my soul, my person

I am simple, I am exceptional
I am everything, yet nothing at all
I am the Creator and the creation
I am the God and the worshiper
Serving my purpose
In this realm of existence, for the time being...
Just as I light up a candle

Universal Souls

When your nationality becomes Universal
& no longer the country where your mother birthed you
When your race becomes Universal
Instead of whatever culture that raised you
When you see me as you see you!
& see yourself as you see God!!
Can you imagine such divine 'civilisation'??
Did you grasp my visualisation?
The Universe is my home...
The dust of the ground, its grass
The little ants and their babies
We're like soul cousins
Are you aware?
The wind and the air
Constantly caressing my being
the rays of the Sun recharge
I couldn't be more grateful for its light
Or is it might?
Mighty of a God to identify
Understanding what it means to say
Namaste to all nature
Inner-standing the meaning of existence
Over-standing that the ability to master oneself
Is to master ALL things...

Who Am I?

Creator & creation
The God and the worshiper
Everything yet so evidently nothing at all
I am the vessel, the potter, the clay…
It's maker, its seller & the buyer too!
Pen, papers,
A story and the writer itself
Eye am the path and I the traveller
I am light and darkness…
projecting all the colours in between…
A sweet reflection of you
I am who Eye am

Namaste

Oh You Holy, Holy Spirit
Holier than whole
Grow within me
Beautiful Soul
Ruler of the Universe
A single drop of water is but this world
This Soul is so much more
The reason I breathe
The reason I love
Everything is nothing
And nothing is All
Grateful for Your presence
Grateful for my own
Guide me deeper
May I drink & heal from Your hand
May I stamp & seal this letter
Allow it to flow up to eternity, infinity
As this incense burns
You are still my inspiration
My God
To think Your thoughts
Feel Your essence
Be Your Soul
Ever so grateful
So glad I am Yours
This is my drunken love
Creator and creation
Together as One

ALL is All

(CLEANSING BATH)
I am who I am
Raw essence within
Herb of the earth
Aiders of ours...
Fulfilling your part
Cleansing me
Protecting me
Feeding me
Fertilizing my mind
Bringing clarity to my Eye
Grateful Great-full Grateful
To immerse in this purified water
Tasting the flavours of the earth
The scent of this burning sage...
Each sound of my chakras vibrations...
Overwhelmed being... being experiencing...
Ecstasy with ALL
Appreciate everything!
Appreciate equally the nothing!!
For ALL cannot be All
Without the small
Without the nothing...
Indulge in Eye
Eye indulge in ALL
I be You
Th-ankh-ing The Elements

I Hear it Now

I hear it
I've been fighting it
Still attached
To fully enter the wisdom
I must comply with its laws
However, much I do it for them
This language isn't theirs
To do it right, is to do it occult
In the quiet
Accept the alone…
The ghosts
Hence the quotes
The hidden questions within questions:
Who came first, the chicken or the egg?

Must Develop the Soul

Mind Burpees
Soul Yoga
Happiness Stretch

Life & Death Inspires

Energy never dies
Why must these scriptures expire?
May Eye rebirth in matter
To find comfort in our past greatness
Accomplished
In death also...
Having mastered the soul in life,
Generating the Sanskrits rooted
Through each root of the tree and crown of life...
A purple indigo pulse...
Pulsating through all existence
Skips none – not even the blind;
The sceptical, nor the fearful...
We are One
All united as well as separated
Beloved brother:
An existing breathing reality
Eye as I cannot fulfil
Although so perfectly I do through you...
Beloved sister:
Likewise, an expanding Soul maternity
Without you, how would Eye
Birth and raise all these Suns ...?
Beloved Suns & Moons

You are the light
Which illuminates me to write...
Without your being experiencing
What purpose would there be
For each essence of this Sanskrit?
Humanity you are the beat of the Universes heart!

Laura's Poem

Some believe what they see
While others love what doesn't yet exist
Perhaps it always did
As the eggs of your offspring
Were placed in you as you received your first heartbeat
If to see your wasted seeds
The physical pain equals to a Soul who seeks
What's rightfully meant to be
Essence can only be what already is
Everything and everyone serves its purpose
Whether or not you'd agree
When that seed fertilizes and fulfils
Now here is all you wanted
Except you had to idea of what to expect
The bad is worse than you thought
And the good is greater than you could imagine...
To withhold the power of life and creation
Hardly realizing the womb is a portal to our realm of existence
Hence the peace, the nausea and troubled dreams
The cravings and emotions, an overwhelming sense of purpose
The body naturally prepares for the greatest confrontation of its life
Pain
Excruciating bone breaking
Pain
How do you describe a day in your life?
Where you went so close to death to bring forth life?
Delivering your lifeline

I smile, because maybe mothers do die
And instead of coming back to life, they're rebirthed
As each and every woman gives birth...
Holding this brand new little person
Takes you to a primitive level of consciousness
The simplicity exposes the vulnerability
By the human sound of your baby's cry
One cannot not stop nor hurry the growth
Learning to love without any control
Experiencing the power of all these undeniable Universal laws
If you ask me what for?
I can tell you of the morning kisses
The tight hugs, runny noses or the lullaby songs
When you walk in a room and your baby claps
Excited to see you, all he can say is:
"Mummy, mummy, mummy..."
How do you respond to such genuine admiration?
It's so clear no one can kiss it better...
A part of you, with a life of their own
Creator of creators
Queen of queens
Mother of all mothers
You are the Goddess of all Goddesses

Womb Shades

Before she brought forth light
In deep darkness she had to dive in...
The light had rather been an illusion
Which separated her from her own inner
So purposefully, painfully, persistently
The dark dragged her back into her own darkness
Hailing hells,
Burning in flames...
She had to remember how she birthed her own God
In darkness...
Where stars shine their brightest
At each bowing of the earth
Earning her light, ever so illuminated
Love & peace contaminated soul
Had not – overcome her darkness...
Rather embrace her truths
Connect back to the true colour of her womb
Embrace once again the darkness of above
As above so below
As the firmaments of above so her womb...

WombMother Speech

I gave you breath
Although you insist on praising life…
I gave you lungs to embrace the airs
Yet you despise the spirits
Mix them with Nicotine
I gave you death
That you may rest
In between bodies
But you cry, scream and shout desolately
Missing completely the opportunity
Of reincarnated reconnection
Whilst we mourn
We stamp a mourned and gone
Upon them
How could you even begin to know yourself?
Before you venture on seeking a Supreme
Until you value breath…?!
Who made you pure… consciousness?

Only the present moment requires your undivided attention

I'd trade all knowledge, technology
Just to remember what is like to
Own the moment...
Yes! A constant passing moment
A moment between the past and the future;
Something between a lie and a story...
I don't want to own something that I must pay for it monthly!!!
To distract me, entice me
What else do you want to sell to me?!
I tried to give it back
Now the small writings of the terms and conditions apply
Means because I signed it
By their terms I must abide...
Pay them my money with time;
Whilst using their service also spending my mind...
The system will always protect who created it!
Who protects me I ask??!!
Eye and I is all I find...

It is not because it rings, that it must be answered...
A text doesn't need response either...

This moment does
require
My undivided attention...
Living an indigenous life in the city!!!

Soul Sanskrited

All Eye type comes from within the soul
All Eye share with you has a purpose
Whether you grasp it or miss it
Soul speaks, the fingers move accordingly...
I am who I am as Eye be...
Stop Scrolling... Read.

God's dreams are really just prophesies!!
Learning the worlds ways fulfilled nothing in my Soul
Embracing my own showed me I was born full & filled
It's time to pour.
A Diamond,
Slaving over Gold...
A lion hunted like a gazelle cub!
Kings and queens
Striving to survive as Sheep
Spending all of our royalty
Trying to live as fish
No wonder we can't breathe...
I rather be shepherd in a land of Sheep
Than be Sheep in a Land of kings!!
You can't be a Master when your master isn't you!!
We can deviate from the truth,

We can fool the sheep or realise we're the fooled sheep...
Truth needs not speak
For it already owns its own certainty.

My wishes for you are of much knowledge of the Self, Self-love,
acceptance & understanding.
You are Perfect beloved
Eye wish you Magic, I wish you Mastery.
Eye wish you Peace, I wish you Poetry.

Fear can be so very Crippling...
As if the Sun doesn't walk on Water at each rise...
Child Of the Sun we walk on any fear like water!!!

Never despise your tears beloved...
Little do you know; their salt is fertilizer to your dreams...

Everyone is chosen, a few choose themselves

Oh my,
What is a King to a God?
What is the Alchemist to its Magic, if not a Slave?
A child to its mother
The mother to its child...
Is creation a slave of its creator?
Or was thy creator slaved into creating Thee?

Eye Wish You Peace, I wish you Poetry
Soul Sanskrit

Indi Writes

About the Author

Indi Writes, natural healer, meditation guru and coach is on a quest to provide individuals with the courage and compassion they need, to heal and transform their lives through poetry. Indi runs her spiritual healing business ***Womanhood2Goddesshood*** and through exclusive spiritual coaching and meditation, assists individuals in finding and identifying with what their soul truly seeks.

www.ingramcontent.com/pod-product-compliance
Ingram Content Group UK Ltd.
Pitfield, Milton Keynes, MK11 3LW, UK
UKHW021829270726
14058UKWH00001B/45